I0016703

Enyo Markovski

The Laws of E-Commerce Project Management

-Effective Books-

"The book is an excellent user-guide for effective and modern e-commerce project management. Enyo Markovski created a brief and very exact overview of all aspects a modern project manager should consider."

Rico Neitzel (CEO) Buro 71a

"Enyo Markovski's book is a great base for successfully executing e-commerce projects. The book covers all areas of project management and applies them to the specifics of e-commerce. The author's broad experience is condensed into easy to remember laws which should guide each e-commerce project."

Frank Reinartz (IT Manager Gulf Countries), HENKEL ARABIA

"An excellent guide that will help you become aware of a number of issues that are common to those who work very closely with e-commerce projects, and explain in a clear and simple way how to tackle them in a better way. Topics are addressed in an analytical way and get right to the heart of the matter without getting lost in unnecessary verbiage."

Matteo Cordini (CEO) PLAYGROUND CREATIVE WEB AGENCY

"The book describes a set of laws which you must definitely take in consideration when you are involved in an E-Commerce project. Even if you're not actually managing the project I'd recommend this book to help avoid common mistakes.

I like the way the information is summarized, especially funny parts like "riding the death horse of the law of failure." Proper focus, clear priorities and responsibilities together with the other "E-commerce Laws" summarized by the author must help you to avoid riding the "death horse" of the ever changing E-commerce."

Felix Hanos (Senior Developer) NEXT COMMERCE

"Despite the fact that there is a big collection of books in Project Management field, Enyo's book is different. Through field-tested practices for e-commerce project management it enables the readers to achieve practical results quickly and simply. The book is working for me, it is pragmatic and friendly."

Petko Ruskov (Professor at FMI) SOFIA UNIVERSITY

"All the elementary DOs and DON'Ts needed for successful projects with interesting playful and motivating approaches, regardless of the used project management methodology in one condensed hand-book. I really like, that it addresses not only the developer side but also the business owner's view, so that it can establish a common ground and understanding for the whole project. Therefore I think, this book is very useful, even beyond the e-commerce topic."

Andreas Thier PROJECT MANAGER
(SRUM, CERTIFIED PRINCE2 PRACTITIONER)

CONTENTS

Part 1

LAWS FOR IMPLEMENTATION AGENCIES

Part 2
LAWS FOR SHOP OWNERS

Acknowledgments

The book has benefited enormously from the comments of many reviewers. I want to wholeheartedly thank (in alphabetical order): Andreas Their, Christian Dähn, Felix Hanos, Frank Reinartz, Jeroen van Eck, Jon Kowal, Kai Krause, Mariela Vacheva, Matteo Cordini, Matthias Büsing, Michael Hitzler, Nikolay Tzonev, Prof. Petko Ruskov, Philipp Wengenroth, Pierre Neis, Rico Neitzel, Sergey Lysak, Sven Röpstorff, Sultan Khan, Vera Oresharova and Prof. Wolfgang Stark.

I am tremendously grateful to Vaska Karaivanova who did amazing job designing the cover, layout and illustrations in the book.

I would like to thank Sandra Walker for her excellent editorial work, all the help and hard work.

Thank you Vassi for your unconditional love and support, without you this book would hardly happen.

About the Author

Enyo Markovski runs an e-commerce project management company in West Germany, providing services to branch leading companies from Nokia, VF Corporation to HSBC Trinkaus. He has degrees in Informatics, is a recognized Project Manager, PRINCE2 Practitioner and Six Sigma Master Black Belt.

WHY WAS THIS BOOK WRITTEN?

I have always believed that knowledge comes first and results follow. Therefore, when I shifted from ERP to E-commerce software implementation, over 3 years ago, the first thing I did was to look for books and further training specifically on e-commerce project management – up to now I have found none.

Being experienced at ERP software implementation, I used methods for project and service management such as PRINCE2, Scrum and ITIL v3. They yielded very good results, but not completely satisfying ones. The main reason for this was that e-commerce projects are extremely fast and continuously evolving. In order to keep up with these dynamics, both clients and agencies are forced to make prompt decisions and take quick action. Because of this and of the amount of methodology information to initially process, if the stakeholders are not acquainted with the methodologies, it is not realistic to expect them to be effectively implemented.

Practice shows that an effective aid would be a condensed guide on what is necessary in order to achieve e-commerce project targets. A guide based on direct experience of what works and what does not. In other words, what an e-commerce project manager should take care of so that, should everything else not work out, the project would still be a success! This book does exactly that; it is not an overwhelming 300-pages textbook, but a condensed, pocket-size handbook to read and refer to before, during and after a project. To complete the picture, there are printable aids and templates (i.e. functional specifications, budget planning, software and software supplier assessment, etc.), which can be downloaded from:

www.e-chieve.net/download.

"One of the most valuable things any can learn is the art of using the knowledge and experience of others."

Napoleon Hill

NINE THINGS THIS BOOK WILL HELP YOU ACHIEVE

✓ Building effective and committed development teams

✓ Keeping the team motivated and focused until the successful completion of the project

✓ Recognizing poor project settings in the early initialization phase and correcting them

✓ Increasing the effectiveness of project processes

✓ Increasing client satisfaction and loyalty

✓ Always knowing where your e-commerce project stands and keeping control of it

✓ Eliminating chaos and confusion, even when leading a multinational program with dozens of projects

✓ Successfully handling project changes

✓ Sustainably increasing the project's benefits

INTRODUCTION

An e-commerce project is a set of processes and activities, governed by certain principles and Laws. In order to successfully manage E-Commerce projects, a manager must understand and be willing to apply the governing Laws.

This book will provide you with the practical Laws of e-commerce project management and guidance on how to follow them. The book is written from the perspective of Enterprise Solution implementation with numerous international stakeholders. However, the principles and Laws described in this book are 100% applicable for smaller projects and Community Editions. The only difference is in the degree of implementation required.

The Laws laid out in this book were carefully derived from direct professional experience in some of the biggest e-commerce projects in Europe. A few of them were devised easily and smoothly, applying the relevant practices from PRINCE2, Scrum and Six Sigma methodologies, whereby Scrum yielded the most results in the shortest time. However, for the remainder, no existing practices could be applied and most of them were learned the hard way: by trial and error. There are altogether 17 Laws, 12 for e-commerce implementation agencies and 5 for shop owners. The Laws are laid down so that you can apply them in the easiest and smoothest way.

Break them at your own peril.

Part 1
Laws for Implementation Agencies

THE LAW OF WORKING ENVIRONMENT

The environment defines the structure of your solutions

Conway's Law[i] states that "Any organization that designs a system will inevitably produce a design the structure of which is a copy of that organization's communication structure". Therefore, the first step toward producing effective e-commerce solutions and delivering successful projects is an effective working environment.

The working environment lays the foundation for the company's culture and therefore for its vision, goals, structure and standards. The ideal environment for an implementation agency is one that empowers each member's creativity, performance, realization, individuality, reinforces the teamwork and creates a sense of urgency. In this chapter you will find advice on how to create it.

FLAT HIERARCHY AND OPEN COMMUNICATION

People are much more disposed to listening and are much more willing to give their full cooperation when advised by friends and equals, as opposed to being instructed through the dry orders of their boss. The best managers do not manage, but lead their team by example.

One of the best ways to get the most support from your team is to make each member feel personally involved and feel that his or her opinion is important for the company affairs.

The best way to do this is to establish open communication throughout the company. You can use any intranet platform (wordpress, yammer, etc.) and different games to this end.

FEELING OF FREEDOM AND INDIVIDUAL EXPRESSION

For most professionals, and especially for creative designers and skillful developers, the feeling of freedom and the possibility to express their individuality has a very high status on their list of values. It costs nothing to the company but it can make a big difference to the professional and can therefore be very beneficial to an agency to the end of attracting loyal and committed professionals. Here are the steps to achieve this:

- Provide them with the possibility of organizing and desing their own work space.

- Provide them with the possibility of choosing their work equipment. Some professionals are Linux, others Mac or Microsoft users and correspondingly feel more comfortable working with their favorite equipment. Set a budget for the work equipment for each work space and give each professional the freedom to individually set up their work space.

- Stimulate result-orientated work, where employees can define, as much as possible, their working hours. This, of course, should comply with the company's needs and, most importantly, with the project specifics.

- Give the employees the possibility to invest part of their working hours on individual project ideas, outside of their daily duties. The optimal percentage should be 15-20% of their working hours, but you can start with 10%. It may sound unusual but, in the end, it is very profitable and it is result-proven by many companies like Zocdoc, Jarn, Colliberty and of course Google. Try it and it will be one of your best investments in research and development.

Respecting each employee's individuality and their feeling of freedom does not cost extra but creates long term benefits for the company.

SENSE OF COMMUNITY

Individual work may be fine, team work would be better, but community work will stand out! In order to instigate and sustain the highest commitment and results from your professionals, you need to generate a sense of community throughout the agency. In a seminal study[ii], McMillan and Chavis identify the four main components of the sense of community: 1) membership, 2) influence, 3) integration and fulfillment of needs, 4) shared emotional connection. They provide the following example of the interplay between these components:

"Someone puts an announcement on the dormitory bulletin board regarding the establishment of a dormitory basketball team. People attend the organizational meeting as strangers, as a result of their individual needs (integration and fulfillment of needs). The team is bound by their place of residence (membership boundaries are set) and spends time together in practice (the contact hypothesis). They play a game and win (successful shared valent event). While playing, members spend energy on behalf of the team (personal investment in the group). As the team continues to win, team members become recognized and congratulated (gaining honor and status for being members), persuading new members to join and continue the trend. Someone suggests that they all buy matching shirts and shoes (common symbols) and they do so (influence)."

Here is how it would look in an e-commerce project environment and what you can do in order to instigate and sustain the highest commitment and results from your professionals:

- Each community member should be able to express his or her individuality and realize his or her potential toward a common goal. (integration and fulfillment of needs)
- The members work within the same physical space. (Membership boundaries are set), (the contact hypothesis)
- Members successfully complete a project and celebrate. (successful shared valent event)
- In order to successfully complete the project, extra effort and personal investment is necessary (i.e. extra hours, weekend work). (personal investment in the group)
- Members successfully complete the following project and are officially recognized. (i.e. posts on website and blogs) (gaining honor and status for being members)
- Someone suggests that they all buy keyboards, mice and monitors of matching design. (common symbols)
- The members do so. (influence)

MAKE IT A GAME

Today, around the world, the equivalent of over 8 billion[iii] American dollars is spent per year buying virtual products and 3 billion[iv] hours per week are dedicated to playing online games!!! So far, the combined players of WOW have spent over 5,93 million years solving the virtual problems of Azarath. If paid $5 an hour, the online players worldwide would have generated over $780bn of economic results per year. But more interesting is how the gaming industry succeeds in persuading people to invest their valuable time, emotions, commitment and even love in solving virtual problems for no pay, but actually getting paid for it.

There are many factors behind an inspiring game, but here are few elements that have an enormous potential for an e-commerce project management:

- Experience bars measuring progress – Instead of rewarding people incrementally, piece by piece (i.e. payment and bonuses), give them a profile: an avatar. Progress this in tiny increments which they own as they go along.

- Multiple short and long-term aims – fixing 1,000 tickets is boring, fixing 5 is interesting. Set up main targets, i.e. complete milestone *xyz* by *dd.mm.yyyy*, but also smaller targets, i.e. take part in 5 meetings, give 2 presentations for the transfer of knowledge, do 2 database performance optimizations. Break things down into tiny collaborative slices.

- Reward effort – Team members get credit for everything they do; they get credit for trying! Do not punish failure – reward effort. The rewards can be of high symbolic and low material value.

- Concise, frequent and clear feedback – People cannot learn if they cannot associate consequences with actions. In games, after achieving a goal, you go up a level. After a successful project, members do not (yet) get: +1 on coding, +1 on creativity, +1 on consulting, etc. Make it simple and easy to understand.

- The element of uncertainty – this is a neurological gold mine. A known reward excites people but what really gets them going is an indeterminate reward; with the right level of indetermination, where they do not know whether or not they will be rewarded. When people cannot predict something, they want to go back to learn more.

- ✪ The biggest turn on for people is other people – Doing stuff with their colleagues/peers, collaborating with each other. To team up, to compete! They need to co-operate in order to win and they feel responsibility to the team – they cannot let the team down.

- ✪ A gentle way to start is to play games – Games generate social fabric. Even if you lose, trust is built. When they play the game, you assume that they will spend their time, play by the rules, value the same goal and stay until the end. I remember when Star Craft 2 was launched. The whole team got it, including me. On Fridays, we played until 4a.m. It was a special experience, an ice breaker on another level.

A playful approach and a game captures the imagination, boosts learning, inspires creativity and projects the team work to a deeper level, which ultimately results in better overall team performance. Learning to make use of these proven techniques to truly engage people can bring astonishing results for the team and the whole organization.

SENSE OF URGENCY

You can only elicit the best results and the most satisfaction for you and your team with a proper sense of urgency. Creating a sense of urgency will hone the focus and motivation of your team, making them more productive and ultimately happier with their work. However, be careful not to push them over a healthy limit, because you may cause overstress and burnout. The appropriate amount of stimulation, as defined by the Yerkes-Dodson Law[1,v] can be seen in the image on the top of the next page.

---

[1] *The Yerkes-Dodson law is an empirical relationship between arousal and performance. The Law dictates that with physiological or mental arousal, but only up to a point.*

Image 1

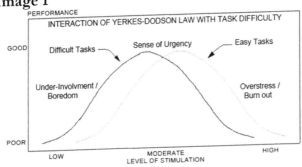

The best way to create the appropriate sense of urgency is to assign tasks with short timeframes – 12 to 16 hours for development and 4 to 8 hours for testing. The more monotone the task is, the shorter the timeframe should be. This way you will avoid boredom and create a sense of urgency; the members will receive prompt feedback and be able to improve; further, you will ensure excellent stage and quality control and ultimately increase the effectiveness and satisfaction of your professionals.

PROPER COMPENSATION

Well, the title is self-explanatory. The company can be great, unique, it may have implemented all the right steps, but if compensation levels are lower than the branch average, the company will have a hard time keeping the professionals in the long-term.

All in all, if you want to create first class solutions, then you need to create a first class organization to deliver them. The first step towards this is to establish a proper working environment in which to promote a flat organizational hierarchy, open communication, the appreciation of each person's individuality, a game approach toward services, a sense of community and urgency.

THE LAW OF BUSINESS PROCESSES

The ship's rudder and compass

An implementation agency's Business Processes are like a ship's rudder and compass; you **must have** them in order to be aware of where you currently stand and of how to move forward to achieve the e-commerce targets.

THE RUDDER

All agencies are different, with different visions and needs, but there are some common must-have business processes.

Before listing these processes, here is a definition of what the optimal process should look like:

It should be clearly represented, with the help of a diagram, including its basic components – inputs, system and outputs; a software tool like MS Visio or any other[2] can be of help). It, should define the exact steps, their order, dependencies, employee responsibilities and timing and be standardized.

The best way to improve your organization is to continuously improve its processes. When an issue (buggy functionality delivered to the client) arises, the first thing to do is to check if the process was followed; if so, then the process should be improved to avoid further common issues in the future.

If the agency is implementing software solutions, these are the minimum business processes that must be Defined, Measured, Analyzed, Improved and Controlled (DMAIC).

---

[2]*For more tools, check: http://en.wikipedia.org/wiki/Diagramming_software*

- Creation and approval of software specifications
- Estimation, budget and quotes
- Software architecture
- System infrastructure
- Software development
- Quality assurance
- Deployment
- Change requests

If the agency is supporting software solutions, these are the minimum business processes that must be DMAIC.

- Infrastructure
- Service ticket creation
- Ticket estimation
- Software development
- Quality assurance
- Deployment

So far, the minimal business processes necessary for an agency to operate have been listed: the ship's rudder. Next, let's define where the ship is and where should it go.

THE COMPASS

Now, you will Measure, Analyze, Improve and Control the ship. This is the MAIC part of the DMAIC acronym – this is your compass. The key point, here, is to define Key Performance Indicators (KPI) for each process. In e-commerce, the KPIs measure the effort, time and quality per task. For example, let's take the Quality Assurance process. Here are some possible KPIs:

- Bugs found during in-house testing

- ☯ Bugs found by the client (after in-house testing)
- ☯ QA Effort efficiency – this is the rate of the expected versu the actual QA effort needed
- ☯ QA Time efficiency – this is the rate of the expected versus the actual QA time needed

After the KPIs are in place, you can start to Measure and Analyze them to find out where the ship is and where it is going. If the direction is not up to your taste – i.e. there are too many bugs found by the client or the QA time goes above estimate, you can Improve it.

The structure of improvement is very simple; an output can be changed only by changing the input or the system. Therefore, the project manager can take a closer look at the task's execution and, if necessary, collect more KPI data and make adjustments correspondingly.

These can consist in changing or eliminating a process' steps or inputs. For example, if the testers are using Macs and have to start using a Virtual Machine every time they test browser performance on IE 6/7/8, it might make sense to get an old Windows machine for browser testing purposes. The best piece of advice here is to use the 80/20 rule. In the real life, almost always 80% of the problems or benefits come from 20% of the work; 80% of delays are due to 1 or 2 tasks, 80% of client dissatisfaction is due to 1 or 2 factors (i.e. performance, delay), 80% of performance issues are due to 1 or 2 settings, 80% of clients satisfaction can be boosted by 20% more in-house testing before delivering, etc. Thus, by using the 80/20 rule, you will avoid the complexity and interconnection between KPIs and create improvements that will not only be efficient, but also effective. Sometimes, less is more.

Now, knowing where you are and how you can change the direction in which you are heading gives you back Control of the ship so that you can steer it into calm waters, when necessary.

If an agency wants to grow and stay in business, sooner or later it must get its rudder and compass. In every e-commerce project there is a rush hour time, in order not to get lost, you and your team need defined business processes related to your project work. This way, you can handle peak workflows, always have a safe haven to return to and improve the effectiveness of your organization.

The Law of Responsibilities

People must own their tasks

Very often, a highly skilled professional has many responsibilities, from time to time he or she is the main developer, the software architect or the project manager, shifting whenever and wherever there is a crisis throughout different projects.

In theory, a professional should be able to carry out each of these tasks; however, in practice, a professional is truly that in only one area. Thus, shifting him or her from task to task will not make the best use of his or her full capabilities and skills; and that is just the smaller issue. A bigger challenge is that, this way, chaos is unleashed throughout the company. Yet, the biggest challenge is that, in the end, none of the tasks will be properly executed. This, in the e-commerce software industry, is worse than doing nothing at all. Execute the tasks halfway or incorrectly and this will eat up the company's resources, the client's trust and the team's motivation!

When chaos is unleashed, nobody will have any idea of who is doing what and tasks will be shifted back and forth. Be aware of such a scenario, as this situation can suit some members of the organization very well, and they will do their best to elude changes; chaos is a great place to wash one's hands and to avoid responsibility, but it is very bad for the company and, ultimately, for the client.

Companies dedicate a lot of energy to trying to counter the effects. Dozens more calls and meetings are organized and hundreds of emails involving lots of people are sent. Have you ever received emails with these titles: FW:FW:RE:RE:FW:RE:

Important!...? Then you know what I am talking about. The issue is that these activities are taking care of the effects and not of the causes. The real cause is poor implementation of the Law of Responsibilities. Here is what you can do in order to remedy this situation.

DEFINE CLEAR RESPONSIBILITIES

The fastest and most effective way to clearly define responsibilities is to create a responsibility matrix. Here is how to do it:

- List the major activities in the project in the matrix rows
- List the stakeholders in the matrix columns
- Define the involvement level, using the ARSI method:

  A – Accountable for successful completion of task

  R – Responsible for completion of task

  S – Supports task

  I – Must be informed about the task

Here you can download a template of a responsibility matrix and use it right away: *www.e-chieve.net/download*. When defining responsibilities, there are the three main areas to consider.

General ownership guidelines

- Each low level task must have only one owner
- The owner is responsible to ensure that the work gets done to budget, timeline and quality standards
- The owner must not necessarily perform the task himself
- Each owner determines who will be involved in the tasks

Team consideration

When defining responsibilities, consider the following from the team perspective:

- Individual availability (in/out house, full/part time)
- Individual capabilities
- Past experience
- Speed of work
- Who can back up for whom on what
- Work styles (alone, in groups)
- Personality conflicts

Project considerations

When defining responsibilities, consider the following from the project perspective:

- Skills needed versus skills available
- Current responsibilities
- Availability of software
- Training needed

UNDERSTAND RESPONSIBILITIES

All task owners must understand their respective responsibilities, their value to the company and agree to take on the task. Use a responsibility matrix and suitable games to determine and communicate task ownership.

LIVE UP TO RESPONSIBILITIES

Once determined and communicated, the responsibilities need to be institutionalized. This means to make sure they are lived up to consistently throughout the company.

The first step is to document the ownership with a Work

Breakdown Structure (WBS) in the project plan, which is public for all project members. Further, project workshops, games or individual meetings can be used to ensure that the responsibilities are being performed consistently.

AVOID FREQUENT SHIFT OF RESPONSIBILITIES

Cross training is useful but software development is not a restaurant business. The time and effort (to provide all access needed, to install systems and databases, to read in the code, etc.) Necessary to shift may prove to be a higher cost than the gain made from the shift.

Developers are employees of higher than average intelligence; however they are human, and human beings need time to adjust psychologically and focus their energy. It may be that you have never thought about or paid attention to this, because no developer will go to his or her project manager saying he or she needs some time to focus his or her energy. However, if you look closer at the development process and compare the performance, you will very quickly become convinced. As a result, the poor performance must and will come out of your project budget.

To achieve maximum professional efficiency, keep the team focused and, to avoid destructive chaos, clearly define responsibilities for all project members, take the time to communicate, institutionalize them and restrain from changing them inasmuch as possible. Employees will value you for removing the plague of chaos from their daily work and will appreciatively identify with their responsibilities.

The Law of Resource Planning

Cannot get it done without developers

Does the quote "Developers, Developers, Developers", speak to you? Yes, you cannot get an e-commerce project done without enough *highly qualified* developers **in-house.**

Realistic resource planning can only be carried out based on the resources that are already in-house. Simple linear multiplication will never work. Hopes of filling the gaps with quick-hire developers and PMs or contracting freelancers will never give 1:1 effectiveness, compared with the current team. The reasons are the nature of a company extension, the Law of Outsourcing and the Law of Resource Planning.

Effective development hours' calculation

Out of an 8-hour working day, there will be an average of 4 to 5 hours effective development work. There are many reasons for this, ranging from the technical to the organizational. Here are few of the distractions that developers meet in their daily work:

- Software updates
- System crashes
- Email correspondence
- Colleague communication
- Internal meetings
- Coffee & cigarette breaks

The point is that there is not really much that can be done about it, except for making realistic estimations and resource planning. Of course, longer working days can be agreed, and this is often the case. Unless you know your team development velocity[3], it is recommended to use the approach suggested here.

Exceeding the current resources

If the project requirements exceed current resources (calculated taking into account realistic development hours) then there are many factors that will affect the effectiveness of the new resources. The biggest influences will be due to the Law of knowledge transfer, the Law of responsibilities and the Law of business processes. For enterprise projects, my advice is to consider 50% efficiency for the first 4 weeks and 75% efficiency for the next 8 weeks. In practice, this means that, for a new developer during his first 4 weeks, there will be 2 hours (50% efficiency from 4 hours of effective development) of effective development per 8-hour working day. This may sound bleak, but it is a reality with most projects, in my experience. In effect, this has very little to do with the ability of the people but mostly with the existing business setting.

See the unseen

There will be technical problems you did not expect: there is no way around it – plan for it. Depending on the project, its complexity and the company's previous experience, there should be an effort buffer of 15% to 30% for a realistic e-commerce project planning.

---

[3]*Development velocity is the work divided by time – effort points (see Part 1, Chapter 6) per stage or iteration.*

CONSISTENCE

When planning your resources, aim for consistency and avoid, in as much as possible, shifts of the project managers and developers across the project.

PROJECT LEADER

The project leader should be first and foremost a project manager. His first priority must be the project scope, including budget, timeline, quality standards, the team's and the client's business needs.

The project leader must neither be the main developer nor the software architect. He must not allow the project, the team and the customer to get bogged in technical challenges and constraints. This will frustrate the customer and erode his trust in the implementation agency. The project leader should be experienced, preferably a certified project manager with strong business affinity, human relations expertise and, finally, technical competence.

IN-HOUSE DEVELOPERS

The importance of having your developers in-house cannot be stressed enough. This way you will drastically minimize response and feedback time; going to the next door or floor to get a developer's feedback takes 10 min., compared to days in e-mail and chat communication. The same applies for the in-team communication. Further, this is the only way to ensure that your project tasks are a priority for the developer. When not using in-house developers, my advice is to calculate a 20-40% (depending on cultural/language differences) loss of efficiency due to communication delays/issues and lack of direct supervision. (More on this topic will be discussed in Chapter 10 – The Law of Outsourcing)

BEST DEVELOPERS TO HIRE

Do you know this type of person: passionate about computers and software since their schooldays, always curious about new technologies and the first to try them? Yes? Then it's likely that you have met some good developers. But add bachelor and master degrees in informatics to this profile and you will find the best developers with the best potential to hire. They will combine passion and a natural talent for software development with scientific thinking and a structured work process. As they will have fought their way up in services and work, they will not be interested in large, quick profits, in company management or project management positions, but in fairness, challenging tasks and a good working environment. The best and possibly only way to get them is to hire them in their last or next to last semester.

HIERARCHY SPECIFICS

Be aware of the company hierarchy and its specifics. Be careful when allocating company executives and shareholders as resources. Their positions in the company are leading ones; it can be challenging for them to roll back to operating (developing, debugging, deploying). You could think of using their operational services only in case of an emergency; however it can still be very challenging. It's just in case of an emergency that the project manager needs his devoted and committed team to put in extra work towards the project's success. Both in theory and in practice it would be a challenge for the project manager to persuade any superior (a shareholder or an employee in a higher position) to put in extra work for any length of time. Hence, keep in mind the company's hierarchy specifics; a successful resource plan is a successfully implemented resource plan.

Finally and to summarize: in order to perform the most realistic planning and avoid unfavorable initial project settings, you need to compute effective development hours, consider loss of effectiveness due to any new, or not in-house developers, calculate an effort buffer and consider staff consistency and hierarchy.

The Law of Knowledge Transfer

It multiplies the power or it cripples the company

Knowledge and know-how are the biggest assets of an implementation agency. People with knowledge and know-how are the biggest resources of an implementation agency. Revenue is generated in exchange for assets and better assets mean potentially better revenue. So, if an agency wants to increase its revenue, doesn't it seem logical that it should improve its assets?

The best thing is that an agency already has the assets and the know-how – it just needs to multiply them. Here is a quick way to do it.

Create a voluntary game out of it

Learning should never be enforced but the result of free will and fun. It should stimulate curiosity and be embraced as a tool for personal development and realization – what it actually is. ILX Group, a leading PRINCE2 training provider, has made use of the context of the snakes and ladders game to create a tool for PRINCE2 examination preparation. The progression and the rewarding of the player are based on correctly answering questions relevant to the PRINCE2 examination. You will find more on making use of games in Part 1, Chapter 1.

Consistent and frequent offers

The transfer of knowledge should be consistent because its value grows with time. It should also be frequent in order to maintain the lead in the daily changing world of e-commerce. The best way to put this into practice is to establish a system of weekly events and workshops for the transfer of knowledge.

STATUS AND APPRECIATION

Establish status enhancement, appreciation and rewards for lectures and students.

Status and appreciation are the second best motivations for a company employee. Sometimes they mean more to an employee than monetary rewards. The best guys in a company, the ones that have the deepest know-how in an area, can be difficult to persuade to share their hard earned know-how. Being the sole repositories of know-how makes them indispensable and non-replaceable – and this is power. Status is power too, a more desirable form of it, one that when used skillfully can boost and ensure the continuous exchange of knowledge in a company. Have you ever seen a CFO, COO or IT Manager of a single person department, happily spending 10- 12 hours in the office, doing the same job and receiving the same wages as ordinary employees? Can you get the same commitment from an ordinary IT or an accounting employee? Big corporations are using this strategy too. Nokia has structured its service departments in such a way that over 70% of their staff is composed of senior to junior managers, executives, coordinators, team leaders and the remaining 30% of senior to junior consultants, specialists and experts. Status and appreciation can be very powerful tools in managing a company and the best thing is that it's free!!! You can use them to entice skillful employees to lead knowledge exchange workshops or prepare e-Learning courses for the transfer of knowledge.

CAN I Philosophy

CAN I stands for: Constant And Never-ending Improvement. This is a constant drive for improvement and moving forward. On one hand, it's a stretching exercise, it means: "If you think you can't, then you must!" On the other hand, it is the Kaizen[4] for knowledge transfer. Imagine you or an employee thinking Oh, there is no way how to achieve the (X) e-commerce project target; now you **must, there is no way around it**! Needless to say, keep it sensible, don't bite off more than you can chew.

CAN I is a great philosophy to introduce to your company, it will greatly boost the transfer of knowledge and will increasingly pay off in the long-term. You can create a CAN I workshop where developers, PMs or both share experiences on how they applied the CAN I in the past week. The group will vote and the Best instance will win. The prize could be football tickets, vouchers for shopping in a client's online-shop, etc.

Imagine that all developers and project managers are as good as the best ones.

What will it do to the company?

Give it tones of flexibility, independence and increased revenue!

What will it do to the employees?

Improve their confidence, self-organization, ability to work independently, empower them and increase their motivation.

What effect will it all have for your clients?

It will reassure them that they are in the best hands; increase their security and trust in their implementation partner and provide higher levels of satisfaction.

Altogether, it will lead to stronger support and trust in any new solutions offered and to long-term loyalty.

[4]*Kaizen – a Japanese word for "improvement" or "change for the better"*

Limiting the transfer of knowledge or even not boosting it will not only limit the benefits, but will literally cripple the company. Concentrating the company's competence into one or two persons can block the development of the whole project, should they become unavailable or overwhelmed. This is especially true when specific extensions or system configurations are carried out without documentation. Effective knowledge transfer can be initiated with a weekly workshop lasting as little as 1 hour and covering step by steps topics such as the most vital development processes (i.e. software architecture, system infrastructure, software development, quality assurance, deployment), making sure that there is no vital piece of know-how held by a single person. Use all the tools you can: games, status, appreciation, extra vacation, material rewards, BBQ on your boat; but get it done!

THE LAW OF SOFTWARE SPECIFICATION

The very key for achieving e-commerce project targets

If there is a single challenge that can alone lead to a project failure, it is the lack of clear agreed software specifications. In my opinion, the leading reasons why software projects fail, next to lack of top management support, is the lack of clear software specifications. In all instances where there are poor or unclear software specifications there are problems – everywhere! The challenge is that writing detailed specifications takes a lot of effort, takes months and the worst aspect is that 50-60%[vi] of it will be wasted as the market and the client's desires change.

WHAT IS WHAT?

In real life, there are many terms related to software specifications, there are: software requirements, software business specifications, software functional specifications, etc. It seems that there is confusion about what means what, and this baffles clients and even agencies. Here is a definition that will help you: software specifications is a general term that defines the complete requirements for a software solution. It is made up of two parts:

- Software business specifications. Here the client should explain the business purpose of the solution, the business needs that it is expected to fulfill and the expected functionalities and behavior of the e-commerce solution in terms of user cases/stories (i.e. "products can be paid via credit cards"). If the client does not have any previous experience writing user cases/stories, it is advisable to hold a concentrated workshop to lay down the ground rules for them and create the first few together.

- Software functional specifications. They are created by the implementation agency and are based on the software business specifications and the workshops with the client. They should describe all technical specifics (i.e. payment provider's APIs for embedding it in the solution), dependences (i.e. product catalog and database structure) and are an essential part of the quote and, ultimately, the contract. Here you can download a detailed template for functional specifications:

www.e-chieve.net/download.

IMPACT ON THE PROJECT

From the very beginning to the very end, the functional specifications have a huge impact on the e-commerce project. To start with, the project estimation and consequently the project quotes are agreed upon based on them. During the project, the project plan is developed around them and during the whole development process it is referred to them for product descriptions and quality requirements. At the end of the project, the e-commerce solution will be tested and approved according to the product specifications and acceptance criteria defined in the functional specifications.

As you see, in each phase of an e-commerce project management, the functional specifications play a vital role. Clear and agreed upon specifications in writing are the key to achieve e-commerce project targets! Use the template that comes with this book, there is a detailed structure to follow to make sure that all aspects of your e-commerce project are covered.

CHANGES HAPPEN – GET PREPARED

Once a project is underway, the implementation and test-ing phases can take from 2 to 12 months or even longer de-pending on the volume and complexity of the project. During this time, a lot of things will turn up that may influence your client's business and the e-commerce solution's specifications. For example:

- Desired functionalities, not described in the functional specifications
- New technologies on the market
- New features in the branch
- Competition's performance and actions
- Client just changed his mind
- Delays by internal parties involved in the project – i.e. warehouse team needs more time to configure the ERP settings for product data exchange, customer services needs more time to populate the product catalog, etc.
- Delays by external parties involved in the project – i.e. the payment integration fails due to payment provider's server issues, SEO recommendations are not finalized as planned, etc.

E-commerce is an extremely dynamic field and, the longer the implementation takes, the longer the list of changes will be. The most effective things to do to prepare for changes are to ensure wireframes and wireframe journeys[vii] for the solution and to adopt agile development approach.

WIREFRAMES AND WIREFRAME JOURNEYS

Changes will unavoidably happen and you need to be pre-pared! The first step is to ensure that you have wireframes and wireframe journeys from the design agency. Wireframes show the navigation, content and functionality of the site. They can be animated by using software or an HTML prototype and thus allow testing of the structure and logic of the site without adding implementation time and costs. A wireframe journey is a group of wireframes that illustrates the steps in a path that the customer can take while browsing your site. A wireframe journey allows the basic functionality of the site to be signed off before it is built.

Agile development approach

Agile development methodologies are a practical solution to the problem of unclear software specifications and the wasteful amount of effort and time spent on predefining them. By using some agile techniques you will ensure that all functionalities will be clearly specified, kept relevant and cost a fraction of the time and effort compared to traditional software specifications.

Agile methodologies adopt the philosophy of The Toyota Way and Six-Sigma in eliminating waste from the processes, which are based on a pull system. This simply means that you pull only as many resources as you need at the time. Applied to software specifications, this means:

- ✦ Prioritizing the desired functionalities in terms of their business value; using the MoSCoW[5] method will help you.

- ✦ Creating an initial effort estimation for the desired functionalities so that, should two functionalities have the

[5]MoSCoW – a prioritization technique used in business analysis and software development. The capital letters stand for: M – MUST have this; S – SHOULD have this if at all possible; C – COULD have this if it does not affect anything else; W – WON'T have this time but WOULD like in the future.

the same business value, the one entailing less effort will have the higher priority as it gives a higher ROI[6].

- Dividing the specifications in stages, based on priorities.

- Preparing detailed functional specifications only for the stage to be implemented. Normally this is done at the end of the previous stage.

For some projects, it may make sense to define the overall functional specifications for the main deliverables (i.e. ERP integration, product import), thus getting a better overview of the project but, at the same time, keeping it short and tight.

CHANGES IN FUNCTIONAL SPECIFICATIONS – WHAT TO DO?

The only thing you can be absolutely sure in an e-commerce project is that there will be changes! This can hardly be avoided, but can be handled in a fair and professional way. Here is a practical approach that takes care of your and your client's interests:

- Always analyze the client's request first. Behind all client change requests there is a business requirement to be satisfied. The client will always have a narrower view of the implementation possibilities than you do. Therefore, identify the business requirement: you may find a much more favorable way (for both of you) to satisfy it. Moreover, this way you will offer alternatives to the client, which will make your work more professional, transparent and fair.

- Estimate the impact of the change and its alternatives (should there be any worthy of consideration). This will include any completed work that needs to be redone and any extra work caused by the change.

[6]ROI – *Return On Investment*

☙ Prepare final estimation results. Independent of the PM methodology you are using, you will always have a list of prioritized and estimated functionalities (user cases/stories) to be implemented, which now need to be amended. An example: let's say that, after your estimation, you found out that the change will impact two completed features each worth 3 effort points[7] and will require an extra functionality to be built-in worth 4 effort points. Altogether, this change will cost your client 10 effort points. In case there are any dependencies on external parties, that will additionally load the timeline (duration of the project), so include them in your estimation results too. Carry out the same process for all the alternatives.

☙ The client makes a decision. Based on your estimation results and proposed alternatives, the client can decide if the business benefits deriving from this change are worth the costs. If so, then there are three options for how to proceed.

  ☙ The budget should be increased by an extra 10 effort points, which can come from the client's change budget. As changes are unavoidable in e-commerce projects and the bigger the project the bigger the chances for changes, it is highly recommended to advise your clients to set up a change budget in their budget plan (see Part 2 Chapter 17).

  ☙ Some non-completed features worth 10 effort points can be replaced with the new feature, thus staying within the budget and still satisfying the urgent business need.

[7]*Effort points – work is much better estimated in terms of effort. Once you have done some work with your team you will have a pretty good image of how many development hours an effort point is equal to.*

- staying within the budget and still satisfying the urgent business need.

- A mix of the two. It may be that, for example, the budget is increased by 5 effort points and some non-completed features worth 5 effort points are replaced.

This way, you will provide your client with a transparent and professional project management, keeping both your interests in focus.

Clear software specifications are vital for the success of an e-commerce project as they are the core of the product to be delivered and are kept in mind throughout the whole project, from the early effort and time estimations to the late testing and product delivery. Therefore, it is important that they are clear, in writing and approved by the client for each piece of work before implementation. It is almost unavoidable that software specifications will change during software implementation; there are two very effective ways to reduce the impact of this risk. The first one is to require wireframes and wireframe journeys from the design agency, thus testing basic functionality before any development is initiated. The second one is to use some agile development techniques for the software specifications and defining detailed functional specifications only for the coming development stage.

The Law of Challenges

Winter always comes - be prepared

The Best immunization against e-commerce project challenges is to anticipate them. Take your time and go over the project plan. Look at all milestones, stakeholders and think about what can possibly go wrong. When doing this, you may find this list of questions useful:

Estimation and deadlines:

- Are the deadlines reasonable and/or realistic?
- Are the deadlines clearly established?
- Are there sufficient resources?
- Do we assume that the current project will closely resemble an earlier similar project? Is this not the case?
- Can the amount of time allocated for the project have been underestimated?
- Can the assumptions behind the plan be wrong? On what basis were the assumptions made? Is this still the case?
- Can the analysis and assumptions have been overly influenced by a charismatic team member?

Technical challenges and know-how:

- Is the software platform the best one to fully satisfy the business needs of the client?
- Is the hardware platform sufficient for the software solution?
- Did we underestimate hardware in scaling/power?

- Has the project manager on the client side sufficient technical understanding?

Communication and documentation:

- Are the functional specifications clear and agreed upon?
- Is there a single point of contact to communicate final decisions?
- Is there smooth, continuous communication among the team members?
- Are there any issues in the communication flow? Can it be that key information is not being shared with the proper parties?
- Is there any team member who feels left out?

Teamwork:

- Are the right people on the team?
- Will there be any staff changes? Will key members leave?
- Can the team become exhausted? If so, are there enough substitutes?
- Does any team member need training?
- Is the team fully committed to the project?
- Are there any possible ego problems in the team?
- Does the team feel appreciated? How do you know?

Business processes and organization:

- Are the internal business processes for software implementation and service clearly defined? Can any of them be optimized?
- Are we prepared for any unexpected changes in time, budget or resources? Is there a buffer for each milestone? What is the current buffer status?

- Is the team burdened with unnecessary work?

- Are the responsibilities in the team clearly defined? Are they carried out? Is there any confusion about them?

- Is the focus of the team spread over different, unrelated tasks/goals?

- How did the development speed of the team change since the last review?

Project direction:

- Are the priorities clear?

- Are there any conflicting goals?

- Does the team have clearly defined goals? Does everybody understand the goals and strive to achieve them?

- Are the transitions between various stages of the plan clear and planned?

- Does the implementation plan have enough flexibility? How do you define "enough flexibility"? What are the exact criteria?

- What is the impact of external parties? If someone messes up, what is the maximum damage that can be caused?

- Is there any interference from an internal or external party?

- How many project impediments were removed since the last review?

Quality assurance:

- Are there any incompatible elements in the plan?

- Are maintenance and support neglected?

- Are there enough quality assurance checkpoints?

- Can it be that incompetence is tolerated for any reason?

◈   Is the security and quality of 3rd party code, including outsourced work, ensured? How?

Go over this list at the beginning of the project, contemplate possible issues that can arise, including worst case scenarios, then prepare for the worst, while hoping for the best. Take the trouble (25 min.) to go over the list every 2 weeks during the project and it will pay off ! It will help you kill the monster in its infancy!

The Law of Information Flow

Clear and complete from the top down

For an e-commerce agency, stopping the flow of information means stopping the lifeblood of the company. Those departments that are not reached by in the flow atrophy and become useless.

Very often information is exchanged at a high level, parties happily agree, but the rest of the team is informed only when it's time to show results – you guessed it: that's too late.

Levels of information flow

The information flow can be disturbed at the following three main levels.

At top management level, where the project is directed, quotes, budgets and deadlines are established, changed and communicated. This communication is the most sporadic and most vital in the project; each piece of missed or misunderstood information can have devastating effects on the project. In order to prevent this, use minutes for all calls and meetings; also use your charisma to convey the importance of the information flow in the company and keep the minutes consistent.

At project management level, where software specifications, project progress and change requests are discussed and defined. This communication happens much more often; depending on the project, in can happen on a weekly basis in so called status calls or, if necessary, a couple of times a week in information calls or workshops with 3rd parties. The biggest problem here is reaching verbal agreements on software specifications and change requests, but then not extending them further to all involved participants. The solution here is again minutes for all calls and meetings and discipline to keep them consistent.

At development level, where project tasks and status information is exchanged in real time day by day. At this level, missed or misunderstood information has the lowest impact. However, this is the most often exchanged information. If there is a hole in the communication pipeline, there can be very costly development and quality deviations, taking the project out of budget and timeline. This is especially true when the resources are not in-house and, even worse, when they are in other countries with different time zones. The way to avoid this is to structure the development team in a way that provides possibilities for easy and direct communication during the daily work. Also, to arrange short and engaging daily/weekly briefings to communicate development progress and challenges.

Minutes for all calls and meetings

Institutionalize minutes for all calls and meetings. The minutes should include: Agendas and To Dos. The Agenda should be part of each and every call and meeting and be sent by the meeting organizer to all participants in advance. Thus, all participants can prepare in advance and be mentally acquainted with the important topics. The To Dos should include the tree **Ws** in e-commerce project management: **What** should be done, by **whom** and by **when**.

The minutes should be published on a common web platform visible to all and, with the aid of a mail and task planner (i.e. MS Exchange Server), the related tasks should be assigned to the corresponding employee's calendar. This duty should be owned by the meeting organizer or someone else on his behalf. This way, at the end of the meeting all relevant employees will know what was discussed, what is to be done, by whom, by what deadline, and the duties owned by each of them will be set in their respective calendars as timed tasks. A further positive effect is that all employees across the company will feel personally involved in the tasks and their importance for the company, which will lead to greater overall duty identification and commitment. This applies to all employees who own a To Do task, even if they did not attend the meeting. The information current in a company always flows top – down, only the feedback flows down – top. Therefore, it is very important to embrace this process first at top management level, then at project management level and finally at development level.

Good "bad news" behavior

When getting feedback from your team that is not positive, behave calmly and do not penalize them for bearing bad news. Otherwise, next time they will just not tell you the bad news. Consequently you will only find it out at the expiry of a deadline, when it will be too late for everybody. Instead, approach it as a shared problem that **we** have to solve.

Informally exchanged information

In practice, there is much important information exchanged en route, during coffee, cigar, lunch and breakfast breaks. At these times, it is not really possible and feasible to take minutes and important information is isolated or even lost. The solution to this is the proper implementation of the Law of responsibilities. This way, if an important topic is discussed and the topic owner is not present, it should be clear to everybody that no effective action can be taken before the topic owner is fully informed. Here it is important to note that only the topic owner should be mailed and not anybody else that might somehow have something to do with the topic. This way, you will avoid organizational waste and sharpen the responsibility focus. On the other hand, if the topic owner is present, it is his duty alone to note it and perform the necessary actions. In this case, it will be very suitable for the topic owner to ask the members for an email on the topic.

PROJECT MANAGER SUBSTITUTION

If a project manager is going to be absent in the short- or the long-term, there should be a handover plan for the substitute project manager to cover the maximum absence duration. The plan should include:

- The tasks and the sub-tasks from the project plan to be done.

- The access to all software and systems required for the successful completion of the tasks. This can be the solution's test, staging and live environment, ticketing system and any other communication tools used for the project.

- The list of people to report to. This consists of internal and external stakeholders. The internal stakeholders are, in most cases, the program manager, COO or CEO of the company. The external stakeholders are, in the first place, the project manager and key users on the client side and, in the second place, the points of contact of all external agencies involved in the project from the client side (design, SEO, marketing agencies, payment provides, fulfillment).

- The list of support people. This consists of the internal and external resources. The internal resources are developers, software architect, infrastructure administrator and quality assurance staff. The external resources are mostly developers represented by subcontracting agencies and freelancers. If external resources are included, it is extremely important that the substitute project manager know the exact scope of their involvement (access rights, booked hours, availability timeframe etc.).

For all contacts, internal and external, it is very advisable to have direct contact possibilities (phone, Skype name) and, in the case of an international project, the working hours in local time. When handing back responsibilities, the substitute project manager should deliver a small report with the status of each sub task. Now, with this structure and a little bit of preparation you will ensure a smooth, professional and painless transition. Examples of contact lists and handover plan can be downloaded here:

www.e-chieve.net/download.

It is advisable to keep track of them from the beginning of the project, thus supporting your day-to-day work and reducing the last working day stress.

Smooth information flow is vital for a successful e-commerce project. It should be ensured at all three levels throughout the whole project. Tools like consistent meeting notes, task planners, responsibility matrixes and contact lists are available to you to make it happen – apply them!

The Law of Outsourcing

Do it right or keep your hands off

Outsourcing is a double edged sword. If executed correctly, it can immensely increase your performance, otherwise, it can destroy your company. Outsourcing opens the doors to highly qualified professionals and great benefits, but also to large security and quality holes. In this chapter, how to avoid the risks and, at the same time, reap the benefits will be discussed.

Why outsourcing at all?

The biggest benefit of outsourcing for agencies is to acquire highly skilled professionals and achieve possible cost reductions of up to 70-80%. In many cases, agencies take over complete projects, without having all the necessary resources at their disposal. A very common example is outsourcing the design implementation (templating) to a subcontractor or freelancers.

Another case is outsourcing abroad, aiming to reduce internal costs and organization. If performed correctly, it can be very effective. Here is an example from Europe: in Germany, an average skilled developer costs a total of €4,500-5,000[viii] per month. In Romania and Bulgaria, also EU countries, an average skilled developer costs €800-1,000[ix] per month. This potential has been recognized for years and many companies are already using it, including branch leaders. For example: the leading web-design and marketing agency Euroweb[x] from Düsseldorf has a R&D center in Bulgaria, HP[xi] has a main Global Delivery Center in Bulgaria, SAP has SAP[xii] Labs in

Bulgaria, etc. By the way, Bulgaria has a corporate income tax of 10% and personal income tax[xii] of 10% – flat rate, which is the lowest in the EU and can also be a side benefit. Nokia moved its technical center from Bochum, Germany[xiv], to Romania. In addition, one of the leading e-commerce producers, Magento, has its professional services in the Ukraine and the platform itself was practically developed in Ukraine. The potential is huge; the question is: how to exploit it correctly?

THE ONLY WAY TO GET IT RIGHT

The only secure and professional way to do it is to establish a branch of your own company in the outsourcing country; hire the professionals on your payroll, have a trusted employee from your company to lead it, instill the company values in them and ensure the proper transfer of knowledge in your local offices. This is the only way to ensure secure, high quality infrastructure and source code for your clients, with the same quality levels that you provide from your headquarters. In my opinion, for project volumes of over €250K, it is definitely worth exploiting the possibilities.

A few words on what can and, to some degree, will happen if you do not do it correctly. What other options are there for outsourcing?

Well, there are basically four options: contract freelancer or subcontracting company, both local or abroad. Maybe the safest choice of all would be to subcontract a local company. This option brings the highest business value for small and medium tasks, when you do not have the know-how or the capacity to implement them with your in-house resources. This way, you will mitigate the risks and reduce the effort related to internal organization and knowledge transfer. The drawbacks with this option are that you will practically have almost no control over the resources. You will never know exactly how much effort they have spent on the project, nor even whether they are working on your tasks right now. You see, even if you have hired dedicated developers, they are still employed by the subcontracting company. If any other project or task is active and has, for the subcontractor, a higher priority than yours, then guess on which tasks your dedicated developers will be working? Further, the costs will not decrease but easily double, compared to the costs of your in-house employees.

Contracting a freelancer to work in-house may be the most efficient solution, especially for the short-term, where you do not have free professionals at the time. In the long term, though, it will not be a realistic solution, as the related costs will be still about 40% higher than those for your own employees.

The benefits of contracting local freelancer or subcontracting companies are that they can work short-term in your house, keeping good communication, efficiency and providing the necessary data security, as they are responsible for data security by Law.

Independently from the costs and quality of the code, subcontracting companies or freelancers abroad without a local representation is too risky and cannot be recommended.

IF YOU GO FOR THE CONVENTIONAL WAY

In case you decide for conventional outsourcing, here are few guidelines you can use to ensure a better success foundation.

- Have crystal clear defined services and responsibilities for both sides. Prepare a detailed Service Level Agreement (SLA), which, in some cases, may stretch to 30-50 pages. If the functional specifications are done professionally, 80% of the SLA work is done.

- Aim, in any case, to agree on fixed quotes! You do not want to pay for their internal work or possible disorganization.

- The best way to outsource work is in isolated, encapsulated units. Less interfaces exist between the outsourced work and yours, less communicational and organizational work is needed and, ultimately, there are less possibilities for errors. Examples for this are mobile and social network applications, extensions, add-ons and so forth.

- Calculate a 10-20% efficiency loss on both sides (outsourced developers and in-house project managers) due to communication and time-zone issues.

- Calculate a 10-20% development efficiency loss due to lack of direct supervision.

QUESTIONS ON SECURITY AND QUALITY

Here are two questions to answer before dealing with any kind of outsourced work (piece of code, software extension or plug in).

- Do you have a process relating to how to test the quality of the code?

- Do you have a process relating to how to test the security of the code?

If the answer is negative or doubtful, then, for the sake of the implementation agency and in its client's interest, it is not recommended to use outsourced work.

Outsourcing can be a great solution to lack of skilled staff and even to improve the numbers. However, if done the conventional way, it comes with a price in quality, security risks and questionable effectiveness due to communicational and organizational issues. The best and only way to both avoid the risks and reap the benefits is to have your own subsidiary in the outsourcing country. This way, you will ensure professional levels of code quality and security, developers truly dedicated to your projects, a lower communication effort and a higher efficiency – therefore the best cost-performance ratio for your company.

THE LAW OF CAPACITY

For a healthy growth, oversell your capacity for up to 30%

E-Commerce is a fast moving, fast growing branch. When the first projects are successfully completed, new and bigger ones will come fast and easy, but there is a catch. If an agency takes on too big a project, it may hit serious difficulties and jeopardize the existence of the whole organization. If a project requires more resources than are available **in-house** at the time, then a high level of attention and consideration is required before taking on the project. A big project can be very attractive, both financially and as a portfolio. However, if it absorbs more than 130% of the available in-house resources – Do not take it! The complexity of the project, the few in-house resources to transfer the know-how and the possible lack of experience and preparation for such projects will clog the company's operation and put its existence at risk. The main reasons for this are:

- The organization's business processes are not designed for such capacity. Their redesign and establishment will involve time and costs.

- Internal knowledge and know-how need to be shared and transferred to the new resources, which also involve time and costs.

- Higher efforts in internal organization and financial management are required, which require even more staff and funds.

An agency can handle the listed challenges one at a time, but not all of them at the same time. In such cases, the best thing to do is to negotiate and sell services (project management, development, consulting and supervision) within the optimal capacity of the company and not take over the responsibility for the complete project. Okay, that's all very well, but what is the optimal capacity, is it different for each company? Correct! Experience shows that for the healthy growth of a company in the e-commerce branch, it should not oversell more than 30% of its current capacity. How do you calculate this? Current capacity can be calculated by the Law of resource planning and can be double-checked with revenue. Adding 30% to the result will give the optimal company growth oversell. For example, if you estimate that, for a particular project, 6 developers and 1 project manager will be needed for 4 months, and you only have 3 developers and no project manager available for this timeframe, then, unless the delivery time is extended to at least 8-10 months – think twice before taking over the project. This may sound uncomfortable and it may be very tempting to take over the project but, in this scenario, there is no way to deliver the project on time and the chances for failure are very, very high!

Like successful businesses, successful e-commerce agencies are built on trends, not on fads. A fad is like a wave in the ocean. It swells up fast and very visibly, but it also collapses very quickly. A trend is like a tide, it is hardly visible, but enormously powerful in the long-term. To ensure a sustainable, healthy growth for the agency, make it a trend and oversell up to 30% of the agency's current capacity.

The Law of Focus

Do not use a spoon to make a hole in a box, use a knife instead

Let's do a real experiment. Take a box and a spoon and try to make a hole in the box with the spoon. Come on, humor me, really take a box and a spoon and try to make a hole in the box. Doing something, experiencing it yourself generates much deeper understanding than just reading about it. Successful e-commerce project managers continuously read and learn but, most importantly, apply what they learn – they take action. Let's do it now!

Image 2

Well, what was your experience? Was it difficult to make the hole, was it even possible? Now let's try a different approach.

Take a knife and try to drill a hole in the same box. Use the same force.

Image 3

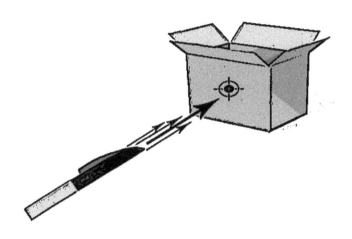

Well, what was the result? Did you drill the hole? Did you use the same force or even less? Could it be that you drilled the hole successfully, with less effort? But why, the box is the same, the effort is the same or even less, what is the "secret"? You see, the spoon dispersed the force onto a wider surface, but the knife focused the energy into one single point. Focused energy was the "secret" that made the difference and will make the difference between a successful and an unsuccessful e-commerce project.

APPLICATION OF THE LAW

The application of the Law can be seen throughout the whole project, and especially during the implementation phase. There are a couple of cases that may necessitate your attention.

The first one is when you have a client with multiple brands on a common platform or different projects with similar requirements. In such a situation, it might be very seductive to carry out the projects simultaneously, using the same resources. It may look like it might work out, save time and even money, but it will not. This impression is an illusion, just like the earth looking flat and feeling still. No, the earth is not flat but round and is not still but in constant movement. Assigning multiple projects to the same resources at the same time will not do you any good.

Another case is when you take over an already implemented project in service and simultaneously implement new solutions for the same client. In such a case, it is crucially important to split the two teams (service and implementation) very clearly in order to keep the focus of each. Otherwise you risk your implementation team to be bombarded with irrelevant emails and issues, and the service team with unknown and non-reproducible bugs, distracting both teams immensely.

Confusion

Take on and put too much on the table at once and the team will end up in confusion, which can lose you control of the whole project.

Confusion and lack of clarity are the biggest time-killers in a project. Confusion is generated mainly by lack of focus. It can also be caused by poor information flow, but even if the information flow is perfect, confusion will be caused by poor focus. Why?

It is to do with Human Nature – the brain can consciously concentrate and focus, **really focus, only on one thought at a time**.

Some people think they can do a couple of things at the same time, but this is an illusion, exactly like the illusion that a single core PC can perform multiple tasks at the same time, like playing music and writing an email.

Have you ever tried to read a book when your mind is occupied with other, currently more important thoughts? After ten pages of reading, you cannot really remember what you have read, but the thoughts were crystal clear. You performed two activities at the same time, but only one was conscious and had your focus at that time – the second was not conscious, it was automatic – on autopilot. The problem with autopilot is that, if the coordinates are wrong, the plane and crew can crash.

Human beings **can really focus upon only one thought at a time**. Understanding and applying this principle will drastically minimize the possibility for confusion and be of huge benefit for the project team and, ultimately, for the whole project.

A rule of Scrum-ban methodology worth bearing in mind is that "no team member should have more than two simultaneous selected tasks and, on the other hand, not all team members should have two tasks simultaneously"[xv]. Every project has to have a patron, a protector, a godfather, like the champion in Six-Sigma; if someone comes and distracts the team with other, secondary tasks, they need to step up and protect the team from dispersing their focus.

The only way to successfully achieve all project goals is to focus on them one at a time. The degree of success will be exactly proportional to the degree of focus. Now, listen carefully, it is not the amount of work or money spent, but it is the focus on each task that will decide the success of the project.

If the Law of focus is violated the teams may end up running around with a very powerful lens on a very sunny day and wonder why nobody can get ignite spark. Finally, keep in mind that the effectiveness of the team increases exponentially with the time it is focused on one project and vice versa.

The Law of Singularity

A slave can have only one master

What would happen if a slave had multiple masters? Every master would have different needs, different desires, would want to go in different directions and give different orders. What would the slave do? Being a good slave, he would run around day by day, hour by hour, minute by minute, trying to satisfy all his masters' desires. Would he succeed in satisfying his masters? Never! Even if he should put in more and more effort and succeed in satisfying all desires at the same time, none of the masters would ever be happy. Why? Each master would have different desires and would wish to go in a different direction. The satisfaction of one master's desire at any one time would take another master away from his goals. In the world of e-commerce, where the budget is fixed and the resources are limited, each extra effort would imply going over-budget and over-time. As a result, not only none of masters would be happy with the direction, but the project might not move forward and even fail. Therefore a slave must have only one master.

Let's take a look at how many people (stakeholders) are involved in a project altogether. On the client side there are: top management, e-com, marketing, customer service, consulting and external parties' teams. Each team has at least 1-2 representatives. This means there are altogether 6-12 people that have something to say about the project. On the agency's site there are: software architect, infrastructure administrator, main developer, project manager and the top management team. This means that there are 5-6 people to listen to about the project. This adds up to 12 communication streams and 72 communication possibilities! Do you see what this can do to the project? What about during the peak stages?

An extra challenge is that although, at a high level, all stakeholders have the same goal (the success of the project) at a lower level, their wishes are different and often conflict with each other.

In the real world, the e-com pushes for best usability and high sales, but the marketing wants cool stuff and brand building. The customer service wants simplicity but lots of functionalities (filters, reports and etc.) backend. The external parties want full implementation of all their functionalities and widgets, but the implementation team wants a fast and stable solution. At management level, the brand (e-com, marketing) wants independence and flexibility, yet top management wants low costs and organizational efficiency, which impose global policies and solutions. At the end of the day, the sun cannot shine on everyone at the same time and not all desires can be met at the same time in a realistic e-commerce project. The agency should encourage the client to obey the Law of singularity and have one project manager, (product owner role) on their side, who will be responsible for the final communication on the client's side. Needless to say, the agency should be an example in this and provide a single point of contact – the project manager for the project.

Of course all stakeholders will be involved in the different meetings, calls and the decision making process. Nevertheless, the communication of the final decisions should be only taken over by the project manager on each side. It is the project manager's duty to organize the internal stakeholders, guide them through the decision process and, ultimately, communicate the resolutions to all parties involved.

All in all, in order to guarantee smooth communication and overall effectiveness across the project, there should be one messenger on each side (client and agency) to convey the final decisions. It is the agency's duty to communicate the Law of singularity to the client and agree on it in advance.

Part 2

Laws for Shop Owners

THE LAW OF SOFTWARE CHOICE

One decision, many consequences

Can one silly software decision affect a whole department or even the entire company? Well, let's check:

- Can performance issues frustrate your customers and drastically reduce the economic results?

- Can product import issues lock your newest collection in the warehouse? Will this affect your marketing campaign?

- Can CMS issues delay your marketing campaigns? Will this affect your revenue?

- Can checkout and payment issues prevent your customers from buying the products? How will this affect your customer relationships and ultimately your revenue?

If the answer of the questions above is positive, then YES, a software choice can definitely affect the entire company. Now, the question is, will it be for good or bad?

To make the best software choice, avoid the marketing slogans and the hype! Great functionalities, a cool look, a bunch of new clients, sparkling articles and news reports, etc; a software can really have great features, but does it actually meet your company's biggest requirements? A thorny question: Do you know your company's biggest business requirements?

For clients employing Enterprise solutions, there are a few business needs that seem to be common:

- Performance – How will the software perform under my current and future (ultimately, all companies want to grow and sell more) traffic volume and product range?

- Marketing – Does it provide sufficient functionalities to support my marketing needs (cross-selling, up-selling, promotions, SEO, etc.)

- Flexibility – Is the software easily adjustable or the core and the database architecture are too complex and require a big effort?

- Usability – Once the software is delivered, how much of the software support, changes and updates can my team do and how much will I relay on external support?

- Stability – Will the software behave stably with my traffic and products volume, on the relevant web browsers?

- Software security – Are there any potential security issues with the software?

- Investment security – Will I be able to get software updates without problems and huge extra costs? How long has the producing company been on the market, will it still be there in 3-5 years?

- Independence – Are there enough professionals on the market? If not, then how will this influence my independence on single suppliers? How will this influence my cost-service ratio? Can resource shortage postpone or even freeze my project?

- Implementation experience – Were there projects of similar size and complexity already implemented with this software and supplier or will my company be the first?

When choosing an e-commerce software solution, use a questionnaire to collect valuable information about future software suppliers and match this data to the business needs of your company. Create a further match between the desired functionalities described in your business specifications and the standard functionalities of different software solutions; this will show you the volume of necessary customization. With these two matches in hand you will have a solid foundation for objective and realistic evaluation. An example questionnaire and functionality match can be downloaded online: *www.e-chieve.net/download.*

A FEW WORDS ABOUT OPEN SOURCE

There is a myth and a misconception about open source. Most companies think that open source solutions are free of charge. Nothing of the sort! As soon as the software is not used 100% as it is, the necessary changes cost as much as a fully paid solution.

This misconception has influenced a lot of companies to issue low e-commerce budgets, just to find out, in the middle of the project, that the reality is different and there is a need to rebudget. Let's go over the list of services that are necessary for setting up an open source solution:

- Definition of software specifications (for more information see Part 1, Chapter 7)
- Software architecture – for some simple solutions, it can be minimal, but still needs to be checked.
- System infrastructure design and set up
- Project management
- Software development
- Software testing

All these activities need to be carried out, regardless of the fact that the solution is open source or paid. The only difference is the license fee for the software. However, for enterprise projects, this does not really matter as the enterprise editions of open source solutions also cost in from €5-15K per year.

What can you realistically expect from open source solutions is the following.

- ☺ Innovation – Open source is an open door for the community to share and realize creative ideas, functionalities and extensions.

- ☺ Flexibility – The code is open for changes, giving the shop owner the flexibility to design their shops with the look and functionalities that their business needs at the moment.

- ☺ Transparency – The code is open, which allows for tracking of what is happening behind the scenes.

- ☺ Independence – The shop owner is not tied to the producer for the software implementation and changes.

- ☺ Slightly lower costs – There are no license fees for the community editions, which in some cases are better and more stable than the enterprise versions. It may sound illogical but, if you consider that the community edition is what makes an open source solution popular, creates the entire buzz and can be directly downloaded and tested, it makes sense.

Choosing e-commerce software can seem challenging for some shop owners, as it involves technical understanding, experience and know-how in the field. Therefore, some owners just go to an implementation agency and consult them as, in the end, the agency deals with e-commerce solutions day by day, has the latest information and ultimately the best software solution for you. Right? Well, not completely!

An e-commerce agency does have know-how and experience in e-commerce solutions, but its opinion is not objective. Why? Because, in order to be successful, an agency needs to narrow its focus. It is very hard and, in practice, not really feasible to own expertise in multiple solutions. Therefore, agencies narrow their focus to a few solutions, which they think are the best or on which their professionals have the most expertise, or, of course, promise the best market potential. None of these reasons, and especially the last two, will objectively help the shop owner in making the right decision. What will help is the following:

- Self information – The shop owner can find out how much a potential supplier meets his business needs. The questions below require no technical knowledge and, in practice, are the most valuable in deciding whether software suits the requirements.

  - Are there other projects of similar size and complexity already implemented – ideally in my branch?

  - How long have the suppliers been in business; both the producer and the implementation agency? Do I know their financial situation? Can I count on their support in 3-5 years?

  - Are there enough professionals on the market? If not, then how will this influence my independence on single suppliers? How will this influence my cost-service ratio? Can resource shortage postpone or even freeze my project?

    Add to this a focused research on users' feedback and comments in forums and blogs on the solutions in question. Type, in a search engine, "problem with …(e-commerce solution name)…" and see the results. These opinions are mostly independent and experience based – you may be amazed how much valuable information you will find.

❦ Professional **independent** consulting – After you have the foundation on your company's business needs, you can get professional technical assistance. Get two independent e-commerce consultants to go over your business specifications and give you their feedback on suitable e-commerce solutions. It is important that neither of them had or has anything to do with the future implementation agency and software producer.

All in all, choosing a software solution for your e-commerce venture is a crucial and difficult task. It can literally affect the entire company and have a serious impact on your business. It requires the highest evaluation because, once set, that's it – there is no cheap and easy way out! E-commerce software choice requires a good preparation; it involves defined business needs, clear business specifications, business assessment of the software solutions and their suppliers, objective user-based feedback on the software's disadvantages, a functionality match between desired and standard functionalities and professional independent consulting. Choosing e-commerce software may be one of the most important operative decisions for your company. Take your time!

THE LAW OF TECHNICAL UNDERSTANDING

Selling or coding? - Managing is understanding

E-commerce projects are specific, technical based projects; they feature specific technical properties, dependencies and their own language. The first step to a successful e-commerce project management is to understand the project.

On the client side, there must be someone with technical understanding; ideally the project manager himself. As much as the agency project manager should understand the client's business needs, the project manager on the client side should have a technical understanding of the solutions to be implemented. Otherwise, they will just speak different languages and the translation will cost extra time and budget, which the client will end paying for.

Commonly, marketing managers, sales managers and customer service leaders are tasked to manage the project as they know the company's business processes best and therefore know what tasks and functionalities the software should fulfill. Correct! This, however, means that they should actively participate in the business specifications definition; the project realization is a totally different animal!

Marketing managers, sales managers and customer service leaders are good at what they do – managing marketing campaigns, sales campaigns and customer relationships. Software project management tasks will just distract them, reduce the effectiveness of their core work and do NO good to the project.

The solution

Get a professional e-commerce project manager. The costs will be covered by the work efficiency of your business leaders and the timely and in-budget implementation of your e-commerce solution.

It may make sense to contract the external independent consultant who evaluated your business specifications and gave you feedback on the software choice.

It is crucial for the project leader to have a technical understanding of the solution to be implemented. This way, he will be aware of possible dependencies and challenges, getting rid of useless discussions, speeding up communication and keeping better control over the agency's activities. Altogether, this will increase the team's confidence, trust in the project and ultimately bring better results in terms of timing and budget.

The Law of Prioritization

First things first

A professor stood before his class with some items on his desk in front of him. When the class began, he wordlessly picked up a very large and empty mayonnaise jar and proceeded to fill it with golf balls. He then asked the students whether they thought the jar was full. They agreed that it was.

The professor then picked up a box of pebbles and poured them into the jar. He shook the jar lightly. The pebbles rolled into the open areas between the golf balls. He then again asked the students whether they thought the jar was full. They agreed it was.

The professor next picked up a box of sand and poured it into the jar. Of course, the sand filled up everything else. He asked once more if the jar was full. The students responded with a unanimous YES.

The professor then produced two glasses of beer from under the table and poured the entire contents into the jar, effectively filling the empty space between the sand. The students laughed.

"Now," said the professor, as the laughter subsided, "I want you to recognize that this jar represents your e-commerce project timeline.

The golf balls are the important things; met business needs (i.e. performance, security, independence, flexibility, etc.), budget, deadlines, top management and team interests; things that, if everything else has failed and only they remain, your e-commerce project will still be successful.

The pebbles are the other things that matter, such as extra functionalities for marketing campaigns (i.e. dynamic banners, interactive widgets, mobile apps, etc.), extra payment methods, more export and filtering options in the backend. The sand is everything else; the small stuff.

"If you pour the sand into the jar first", he continued, "There is no room for the pebbles or the golf balls. The same goes for your project. If you spend all your and your team's time and energy on the small stuff, you will never have room for the important tasks that are crucial to your project.

Set your priorities! The rest is just sand."

One of the students raised her hand and inquired what the beer represented.

The professor smiled. "I'm glad you asked. It just goes to show you that no matter how full your project timeline may seem, there's always time for a couple of glasses of beer with your team and friends."

Now, what would happen if you got caught up in filling the jar with sand and pebbles, focusing on dynamic banners, interactive widgets, special complex promotions and, in the end, there was no place for one of the golf balls – i.e. performance? How would it affect the store, having all these widgets and complex promotions while the site loads like on a dial-up connection from 1995? It would greatly frustrate the customers and they would just leave the shop and hardly ever come back, plus Google would downgrade the page ranking because of poor performance, which would lead to losing more traffic and ultimately sales. This is the case when missing only one of the golf balls – performance. What about the rest?

Let's make our life easier and do it right, the easy way.

- ☻ Define all your business needs.

- ☙ Prioritize your needs, preferably into a maximum of three groups (Must, Should, Could). An unfulfilled "Must-need" will have negative influence with regard to achieving your e-commerce targets. A fulfilled "Should-need" will bring benefits to the project but, if unfulfilled, it will not have a negative influence with regard to achieving your e-commerce targets. A "Could-need" does not really bring any benefits to the project, so we will not bother with it.

- ☙ Communicate the priorities to all stakeholders involved and check their realization.

It is as simple as that and works. As the Spanish painter Salvador Dali said, "It is either easy or impossible" – it is a very true quotation and especially meaningful for e-commerce projects.

As the story goes, it is possible to get it all only if you prioritize! Otherwise, you can easily get too much project at the end of the timeline.

THE LAW OF FAILURE

Admit it promptly and move on!

Failure happens, it happens everywhere, in every branch and in every company. It should be expected and accepted. Some projects do not go the right way. When this happens, admit it promptly and move on. Do not try to fix it or to reorganize and struggle to save the situation. It will drain more and more of your time and resources. Identifying a mistake and doing nothing about it is bad for the project and ultimately for your career. A much better approach is to admit a failure early and cut your losses.

The biggest identifier for an e-commerce project failure is when, after the second postponement of the launch date, the solution is still not live. These are three failed launches, which means that:

- Most probably, a couple of things went wrong on all sides. In such a case, the fault never falls on one side, but on many – i.e. the client's timeline was a bit optimistic, the implementation agency's resource planning was unrealistic, the 3rd party software providers had technical issues, the design agency supplied an incomplete design, etc. Although the challenges may appear technical, the real causes are political and managerial. The slightly optimistic timeline was set by the client's top management in order to boost the revenue numbers or another corporate goal. The priorities, where the resources are allocated and the technologies to be supported are identified, based on the overall wellbeing of the implementation agency, 3rd party software providers, design agency, etc. and not on the single project. At the end of the day, all the stakeholders were approved by the client's management.

⊛ Most probably some or all of the Laws in this Part were violated.

As a result of this, the teams on both sides lose their trust and belief in the project and its management and will not commit to the level necessary for the successful completion of the project.

The best advice to give is to follow the tribal wisdom of the Dakota Indians, passed on from one generation to the next, which says:

"When you find that you are riding a dead horse, the best strategy is to dismount."

But in e-commerce project management, because heavy investment factors and agendas are taken into consideration, other strategies are often tried with dead horses, including the following:

⊛ Buying a stronger whip.

⊛ Changing riders.

⊛ Threatening the horse with termination.

⊛ Appointing a committee to study the horse.

⊛ Arranging to visit other sites to see how they ride dead horses.

⊛ Lowering the standards so that dead horses can be included.

⊛ Reclassifying the dead horse as "living-impaired".

⊛ Harnessing several dead horses together to increase speed.

- Providing additional funding and/or training to increase the dead horse's performance.

- Doing a productivity study to see if lighter riders would improve the dead horse's performance.

- Declaring that the dead horse carries lower overhead and therefore contributes more to the bottom line than some other horses.

- Change the requirements from "riding" to "moving" and issue a new development contract for it.

- Instituting an affirmative action policy to hire more dead horses, on the basis that they would be fine if only their lack of skills were not held against them.

- Rewriting the expected performance requirements for all horses.

- Form a quality circle to find other uses for dead horses.

- Purchase a product to make dead horses run faster.

- Appoint a special team to revive the dead horse.

- Patent the horse as soon as possible.

- Hiring outside contractors to ride the dead horse.

And, as a final strategy:

- Promoting the dead horse to a supervisory position.

The message in this listing is clear. Unsuccessful e-commerce project managers do not let it go. They bite into something and do not see that the situation does more damage than good.

Successful e-commerce project managers let go.

Wall Mart's chief executive said, in a Business Week article: "If you learn something and you do something, then you will probably get credit for it. But woe to the person who makes the same mistake twice."

Mistakes and failure happen all the time and are part of the path to excellence. As the Nobel Prize winner Nils Bohr said: "An expert is a man who has made all the mistakes which can be made, in a narrow field". In case of failure, the most effective solution is to recognize it, cut losses as early as possible and LEARN! Go through the Laws in this book and compare – Learn. If the business needs are still open, then use your hard learned know-how and design a new project taking care that you and your stakeholders are obeying the Laws of e-commerce project management.

THE LAW OF RESOURCES

No money, no funny

Resources are the fuel of the project. If the fuel runs out half way through the journey, it does not matter how good, special, accessorized and customized the car is, it will cut out in the middle of a lovely landscape.

Having too much project at the end of the budget, means that the project in its initial settings is failed. Well, this does not certainly mean it's the end. Depending on the project situation and its importance, it can be rebudgeted and given a second chance; nevertheless, this is definitely not a desirable situation for the project manger and the team. It certainly can be avoided with a careful, realistic budget estimate.

REALISTIC BUDGET ESTIMATE

To do a realistic budget estimate, you need to have a clear overview of the tasks. Then you will need to compute the effort for each of them, which is normally calculated by the "working days" x "cost per day". If this is your first project, it is recommended to use the services of a professional, independent e-commerce consultant for feedback.

In the table below, you will find an example of an e-commerce budget calculation. A printable version can be downloaded online:

www.e-chieve.net/download.

Tasks	Days of work	Price per day	Cost of task	Notes / Assumpptions
Information architecture[1]				
Infrastructure architecture[2]				
Decision supports[3]				
Product catalog design and import				
Customer support areas of the site				
Design of the site[4]				
Graphical work[5]				
Creation of CSS style sheets				
Implementation of design				
Implementation of technical customizations[6]				
Payment methods integration				
Translation files[7]				
Backend configuration[8]				

Tasks	Days of work	Price per day	Cost of task	Notes / Assumpptions
Integration with stock control and ordering systems (ERP)				
Additional widgets and extensions[9]				
Data migration[10]				
Text and media entries				
Testing				
Project management				
Staff training				
Project total				
Project buffer 20%[11]				
Change budget[12]				
Risk budget[13]				
Final total				

1) *Designing customer journeys, modeling products and categories, returning process, etc*

2) Staging, testing and live server, CDN, etc

3) Gift finders, reviews, product guide, compare products, product carousels, etc

4) Including wireframes, possibly xHTML templates for pages and usability consulting

5) Flash, dynamic components, etc.

6) All functionalities that deviates from the standard software and are not listed in this table

7) Designing and processing the translation files (in case of customized multilingual sites)

8) Tax rates, support emails, SEO settings, etc.

9) Facebook, iPhone Apps, SEO and targeting pixels, etc.

10) Any data migration from previous systems. Depending on the project it can be a pretty big chunk.

11) In the practice, 20% buffer is enough to cover unexpected events

12) Sum of money to fund change requests and possibly their analysis

13) Sum of money to cover responses to threats and opportunities (i.e. implement fallback plans)

These are the basic categories in budget estimate and can vary depending on the project scope. Use this table to do your internal budget planning and as a base to compare quotes. If you have calculated over the quotes of your implementation partner, do not rush to cut the budget or allocate it for other tasks. In practice, it is very possible that the agency miscalculated the effort related to the project or was just too committed to take it. This can be a very critical and dangerous situation for the project, especially half way through the journey.

Resources are the propellant for the e-commerce project; if the flow stops, the project stops and, if the resources are exhausted before completion, the project fails. In order to prevent this, all project efforts, including all actual tasks, should be carefully planned, buffered up 20% and possibly include change and risk budget.

Final Words

Simply put, the e-commerce project manager's work is to get the job done and keep everybody happy. This can be only made possible by obeying the Laws of e-commerce project management. If they are violated, the project manager's work becomes mainly a political juggling act with the aim of keeping everybody happy. In fact, the only effect this has is to postpone and deepen the problem – this creates a project debt!

Political juggling alone is not designed for solving problems and, hence, it cannot do so. Science and technology are designed for solving problems and are the genuine reason behind every really beneficial business development and improvement! Science and technology develop solutions, proactively applying and obeying the Laws in a specific field. The Laws in your field have been laid down in this book and it is up to you to use them and successfully organize and manage your project.

As you already know, the e-commerce world is very active and evolves ever faster. It is my assumption that the Laws will remain the same, but the approaches and possibilities to go about them will evolve and improve. To follow the latest improvements and news check out the community forum on e-commerce project management at:

www.e-chieve.net/forum

INDEX

Literature

Friedlein, A. (2001). Web Project Management. San Francisco, CA: Morgan Kaufmann Publishers

Cohn, c. (2009). Succeeding with Agile: Software Development Using Scrum. Boston, MA: Addison-Wesley Professional

Liker, J. (2003). The Toyota Way. New York, NY: McGraw-Hill

Ohno, T. (1988). Toyota Production System. Portland, OR: Productivity Press

Koch, R. (1999). The 80/20 Principle: The Secret to Achieving More with Less. New York, NY: Crown Business

Office of Government Commerce (2009). Managing Successful Projects with PRINCE2 2009 Edition Manual. London, UK: The Stationery Office

George, M. (2003). Lean Six Sigma for Service: How to Use Lean Speed and Six Sigma Quality to Improve Services and Transactions. New York, NY: McGraw-Hill

Krause, K. (2010). Change Management (German Edition). Norderstedt, Germany: Books On Demand GmbH

Microsoft Research (2008). The Influence of Organizational Structure On Software Quality: An Empirical Case Study. Association for Computing Machinery

REFERENCES

i **Melvin E. Conway: Conway's Law**
http://www.melconway.com/research/committees.html
last visited at 04.04.2011

ii **McMillan, D.W. & Chavis D.M.: Sense of Community**
http://www.drdavidmcmillan.com/docs/SOC%20AR-TICLE%201.doc
last visited at 04.04.2011

iii **Tom Chatfield: 7 ways games reward the brain**
http://www.ted.com/talks/lang/eng/tom_chatfield_7_ways_games_reward_the_brain.html
last visited at 04.04.2011

iv **Jane McGonigal: Gaming can make a better world**
http://www.ted.com/talks/jane_mcgonigal_gaming_can_make_a_better_world.html
last visited at 04.04.2011

v **Hamilton L. & Timmons C: Drugs, Brains and Behavior**
http://www.rci.rutgers.edu/~lwh/drugs/chap08.htm#Arousal as Reward

last visited at 04.04.2011

vi Jeff Sutherland: Lessons learned at Google
http://video.google.com/videoplay?docid=87952143087
97356840&ei=GacNS_7yNMfJ-AbfrLnbBQ#
last visited at 04.04.2011

vii Jonathan Briggs: Wireframe Journeys
http://www.jonathanbriggs.com/e-commerce/design-
ing-customer-journeys-lecture-5,766,AR.html
last visited at 04.04.2011

viii Monster Deutschland: IT-Einkommen Deutschland 2010
http://arbeitgeber.monster.de/hr/personal-tipps/
markte-analysen/gehaltsanalysen/it-einkommen-
deutschland-2010-66824.aspx
last visited at 04.04.2011

ix Invest Bulgaria Agency: IT & Telecommunica-tionsFactsheet-March 2010
http://www.investbg.government.bg/upfs/27/08%20
IT%20&%20Telecommunications%20Factsheet%20
2010.pdf
last visited at 04.04.2011

x Frankfurter Allgemeine Zeitung
http://www.faz.net/s/RubCE5E4A7C-
4D514EF49385D627A87356A9/Doc~EAF87CCCA5F
104636893315AE4F52E759~ATpl~Ecommon~Sconte
nt.html

last visited at 04.04.2011

xi Invest Bulgaria Agency: HP Global Delivery Center in Sofia

http://www.investbg.government.bg/index.
php?sid=21&ssid=118&c=200
last visited at 04.04.2011

xii Invest Bulgaria Agency: SAP Labs Bulgaria

http://www.investbg.government.bg/index.
php?sid=21&ssid=118&c=735
last visited at 04.04.2011

xiii Invest Bulgaria Agency: Operational Costs in Bulgaria, April 2011

http://www.investbg.government.bg/upfs/49/Opera-
tional%20cost%20BG%20April%202011.doc

xiv Wikipedia: Nokia-Werk Bochum

http://de.wikipedia.org/wiki/Nokia-Werk_Bochum
last visited at 04.04.2011

xv Wikipedia: Scrum-ban

http://en.wikipedia.org/wiki/Scrum_(development)#
Scrum-ban
last visited at 04.04.2011

NOTES

www.ingramcontent.com/pod-product-compliance
Lightning Source LLC
Chambersburg PA
CBHW060947050326
40689CB00012B/2587